World Book, Inc.
233 N. Michigan Avenue
Chicago, IL 60601
U.S.A.

For information about other World Book publications,
visit our website at **http://www.worldbookonline.com**
or call **1-800-WORLDBK (967-5325).**

For information about sales to schools and libraries, call
**1-800-975-3250 (United States);**
**1-800-837-5365 (Canada).**

**Library of Congress Cataloging-in-Publication Data**

Learning about weather.
     p. cm. -- (Learning playground)
   Includes index.
   Summary: "An activity-based volume that introduces
different types of weather. Features include a glossary,
additional resource list, and an index"-- Provided by
publisher.
   ISBN 978-0-7166-0235-4
   1. Weather--Juvenile literature. 2. Meteorology--
Juvenile literature.  I. World Book, Inc.
   QC981.3.L43 2011
   551.5--dc23
                      2011017693

Learning Playground
Set ISBN: 978-0-7166-0225-5

Printed in Malaysia by TWP Sdn Bhd, Johor Bahru
1st printing July 2011

**Acknowledgments:**
The publishers gratefully acknowledge the following sources for photography. All illustrations were prepared
by WORLD BOOK unless otherwise noted.

Cover: Shutterstock; Image Source/SuperStock; iStockphoto

Corbis Cusp/Alamy Images 33; Enigma/Alamy Images 10; Michael Ventura, Alamy Images 60; Myrleen
Pearson, Alamy Images 60; Ryan McGinnis, Alamy Images 51; Zuzana Dolezalova, Alamy Images 41;
Dreamstime 5, 14, 16, 24, 38, 46, 54; Electron Microscopy Unit, ARS, USDA 33; Mandel Ngan, AFP/Getty
Images 47; istockphoto 10; JSC/NASA 8; Jeff Schmaltz, MODIS Rapid Response Team, NASA/GSFC 42;
NOAA; Mark Boland, NOAA; Shutterstock 4, 5, 7, 13, 15, 16, 17, 19, 20, 21, 22, 23, 24, 25, 27, 28, 29, 32, 33,
36, 37, 40, 43, 50, 56, 57, 59, 61; Tom Tropinski 34-35, 38-39.

# Table of Contents

There is a glossary on page 62. Terms defined in the glossary are in type that **looks like this** on their first appearance on any spread (two facing pages).

# What Is Weather?

Somewhere on Earth right now, it is cloudy and rainy. Somewhere it is sunny. Somewhere it is dark, windy, and snowing.

Weather is the condition of the air at a certain time and place. The weather may be warm and sunny in one place. In another place, it may be cold and snowy. Earth has many different kinds of weather.

Raindrops fall from clouds. Large raindrops fall to Earth faster than smaller raindrops.

On a sunny day, you may feel the warmth of the sun on your skin.

Some parts of the world get much snow. Others get none at all.

On a windy day, you may see the leaves on trees blow and clouds move across the sky.

We describe the weather in many ways. For example, we may talk about the temperature of the air. Temperature is a measure of how hot or cold it is. We may talk about whether the sky is cloudy. We may measure the speed of the wind. We may talk about whether it is raining or snowing. We may also measure how much rain or snow fell.

# MEASURE THE WEATHER

This experiment will help you find patterns in the weather over time. It will give you practice measuring the outdoor temperature.

A **thermometer** is an instrument that measures temperature. It measures temperature in units called Fahrenheit degrees or Celsius degrees.

## MATERIALS

- Outdoor thermometer
- Paper
- Pencil

## DIRECTIONS

1. Ask an adult to put the thermometer in a safe place outdoors.

2. Check the temperature five times a day: early morning, midmorning, noon, midafternoon, and evening. Write down the exact times and temperatures. When did the temperature rise and fall?

3. Check the temperature at the same times every day for seven days. Create a chart like the one on page 7 to record the temperatures.

4. Compare the temperatures for the seven days. Did the temperatures rise and fall at the same times? What factors seem to influence temperature?

| | Monday | Tuesday | Wednesday | Thursday | Friday | Saturday | Sunday |
|---|---|---|---|---|---|---|---|
| 6:30 am | 40°F | 42°F | | | | | |
| 9:00 am | 44°F | 47°F | | | | | |
| 12:00 pm | 46°F | 55°F | | | | | |
| 4:00 pm | 47°F | 59°F | | | | | |
| 7:30 pm | 45°F | 55°F | | | | | |

# Earth's Atmosphere

Long ago, people believed the sky was a roof that stretched over Earth. Today, we know that there is no roof. Instead, a thick layer of air surrounds our planet. This layer of air is called the **atmosphere** (AT muh sfihr).

Earth's gravity prevents the atmosphere from floating away into space. Gravity is a force that pulls things toward the center of Earth. But the air is free to move around near the surface. The movement of air causes changes in the weather.

Thermosphere

Mesosphere

Stratosphere

Earth's atmosphere is
made of several layers. We live
in the part called the troposphere.

Troposphere

The atmosphere extends for hundreds of miles.
Down by the ocean, the air is thick. Up on a
mountaintop, the air is thinner. Even farther away
from the surface, the air thins and disappears
altogether. That is where outer space begins!

Try this!

Try making your own model of the atmosphere. Collect four groups
of beads. Each group should be a different color to represent a
different layer of the atmosphere. Fill a tall glass jar, such as a
vase, with ½ cup of your first group of beads. This layer
represents the troposphere. Then place 1 cup of your second group
of beads into the jar. This layer represents the stratosphere.
Place 1 cup with your third group of beads in the jar. This layer
represents the mesosphere. Finally, place 2 ½ cups of your fourth
group of beads into the jar to represent the thermosphere. The
thermosphere is the largest layer of the atmosphere. You can
tape labels to the side of the jar to identify each layer of the
atmosphere.

# What Is Air Made Of?

Air doesn't seem to be made of anything. It has no color, taste, or smell. You can see right through it. But air is made up of invisible gases. These gases are made up of tiny pieces called **molecules.** Gases are light, but they are not weightless. That is because molecules give gases weight.

You cannot see air, but you can see the effects of air as wind.

For living things, the most important gas in the air is oxygen (AHK suh juhn). We breathe to get oxygen into our bodies. Animals must breathe oxygen or they will die.

On a cold day, you can see your breath. You release carbon dioxide gas when you breathe out.

Only about one-fifth of the air is made up of oxygen. Most of the air—nearly four-fifths—is nitrogen. Plants need nitrogen to grow. Animals also need nitrogen, which they get from plants.

The rest of the air is made up of many different gases. One of these gases is carbon dioxide (KAHR buhn dy AHK syd). Animals breathe out carbon dioxide. Plants use carbon dioxide to make their food. Also, dust and tiny droplets of water float in the air, but they are not part of the air.

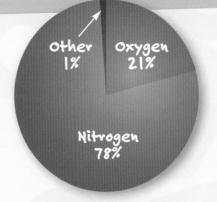

Other 1%
Oxygen 21%
Nitrogen 78%

Nitrogen and oxygen are the two main gases in air.

Try this!

You can see that air is made of something. Turn a glass upside down and push it straight down into a bowl of water. The water will not fill up the glass because air is trapped inside it.

Turn the glass on its side. You will see air bubbles escape out of the glass. Then the glass will fill with water because air isn't taking up space inside it.

# HOW DOES AIR PUSH?

Just as a fish lives in water, you live in an ocean of air. Air is much lighter than water, but it still has weight. The weight of air pushes against you in all directions, even though you are not aware of it. See for yourself how air pushes.

## MATERIALS

- Drinking glass (made of clear glass—not plastic or paper)
- Water
- Piece of stiff, flat cardboard
- Sink or large pan

## DIRECTIONS

1. Fill the glass nearly to the top with water.

2. Cover the top of the glass with the piece of cardboard. (Note: if the cardboard is too soft, or if the glass isn't completely full, this experiment will not work. You will spill the water.)

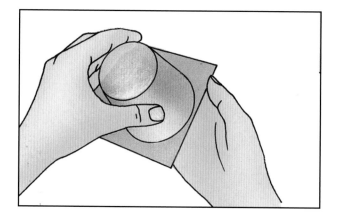

3. Hold the cardboard in place and turn the glass upside down. Do this over a sink or a large pan in case the cardboard slips.

4. Move your hand away from the cardboard. What happens?

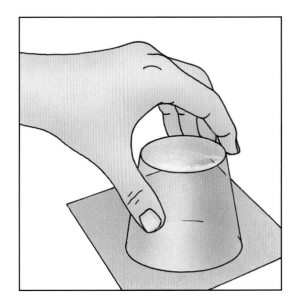

Did you think the water would push the cardboard away and spill out? Several things are working together to keep that from happening. One of them is that all the air pushing on the bottom of the cardboard weighs more than the water in the glass. That weight pushes against the cardboard hard enough to keep the cardboard in place.

The weight of air from the top of the **atmosphere** presses down upon the layers of air below it. This causes **air pressure.** Air pressure can cause many changes to the weather. For example, winds are caused by the flow of air from an area of high air pressure to an area of low air pressure. Scientists who study weather can measure air pressure using a tool called a **barometer.** They use barometers to detect changes in air pressure. In most cases, such changes indicate that the weather will soon change. You can learn how to make your own simple barometer on pages 44-45.

13

The sun gives us heat, light, and other kinds of energy.

# A Sunny Day

What do you like to do on a sunny day? Many people like to play outdoor sports or have a picnic. Swimming is a fun way to cool off on hot sunny days.

Sunlight is important to all living things. The sun gives us light and heat. Animals, plants, and people depend on this energy from the sun. Plants use sunlight to make their own food. Animals get their energy by eating plants. Even animals that eat other animals get their energy from plants. And all of the energy in plants comes from the sun.

Animals and plants need sunshine to survive.

As the sun moves through the sky during the day, your shadow changes shape. On a sunny day, have a friend help you capture your shadow at three different times to see how it changes with the sun. Pick a spot on the sidewalk and stand on it in the morning, at noon, and in the late afternoon, while your friend traces your shadow in chalk. How did your shadow change throughout the day? When is your shadow the longest?

Sunlight is the most important influence on the temperature of a place. The more sunlight an area gets, the warmer it is.

The **equator** (ih KWAY tuhr) is an invisible line around the middle of Earth. Areas near the equator get lots of sunlight. These areas are hot. Areas near the North Pole and the South Pole get less sunlight, so they are cold.

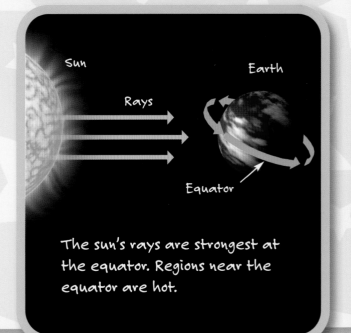

The sun's rays are strongest at the equator. Regions near the equator are hot.

# A Windy Day

Wind can be weak or strong. It takes only a weak wind to blow the soft, fluffy fur of this dog.

The sails on sailboats are designed to capture wind. This pushes the boat forward.

Wind is moving air. The wind moves over the land. It rustles leaves on trees. In a storm, it whirls and roars. Wind can change a cloudy day into a sunny one.

The wind blows because different parts of the **atmosphere** have different temperatures. When sunlight heats the air, it makes the **molecules** of gas in the air move faster. The molecules spread apart. This makes warm air lighter than cool air. As a result, warm air rises to float above cool air.

The push of wind helps to lift a kite into the sky.

As warm air rises, cool air from other places flows in to replace the warm air. This moving air is the wind. When you feel the wind blow, you are feeling the movement of cooler air. This air is pushing in to take the place of the warm air that rose up into the sky.

What happens to the warm air? As it rises, it cools. When the air cools, it becomes heavier. This cool air sinks back to the ground. There it takes the place of warmer air, and all the same changes happen over again!

On a sunny day, the air above land near the ocean is warmer than air over the water. The warmer air expands, becomes lighter, and rises. The cooler air from the sea moves in, producing a cool sea breeze.

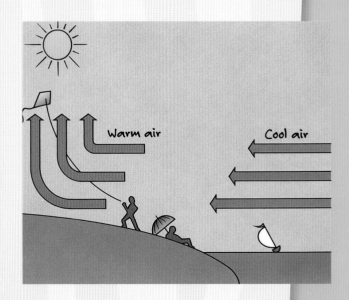

Warm air

Cool air

# MAKE YOUR OWN WIND SOCK

A wind sock can tell you how much the wind is blowing and in which direction. Use these directions to make your own wind sock.

## MATERIALS

- Long sleeve from an old shirt
- Thin, flexible wire
- Stapler
- String

## DIRECTIONS

1. Measure the wire to fit around the shoulder part of the sleeve. Form the wire into a circle to fit the sleeve opening.

2. Tie one end of the string around the wire.

3. Staple the edges of the sleeve over the wire. (Be sure the staples are close together.) Leave the long end of the string hanging out. Now you have a wind sock.

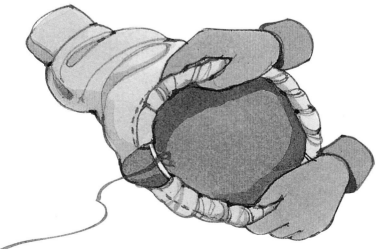

4. Tie the wind sock to a tree or post.

5. Watch the wind sock for several days. Some days the sock will hardly move. On other days, the wind will make it stand nearly straight.

↑

Wind socks are often placed in open areas where they can capture the wind.

In which direction does the wind tend to blow most often? Move your wind sock to different locations. Is one place around your house windier than the others?

# What Are Fronts?

The air moves around in large bodies, or masses. Conditions inside each mass of air are much the same. Inside one mass, the air might be cold and dry. Inside a neighboring mass, the air might be warm and wet.

The boundary between two masses of air is called a **front.** Fronts move over time. A cold front will bring colder air with it. A warm front will bring warmer air.

When two fronts meet, it can cause stormy weather.

Try this!

What happens when a front moves into your area? When the weather **forecast** reports that a front will move through, observe the changes in weather. Does the temperature get hotter or colder? Are there strong winds or rain? Does the air feel any different after the front has passed?

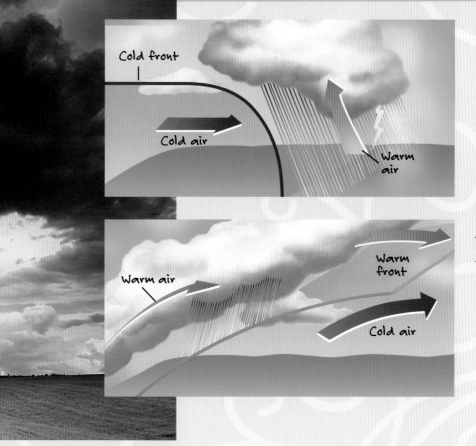

Cold front

Cold air

Warm air

Warm air

Warm front

Cold air

A cold front (top image) occurs when a cold air mass pushes against a warm air mass. A warm front (bottom image) occurs when a warm air mass enters an area and pushes a cooler air mass out. When there is a big temperature difference between the air masses, very bad weather can result.

Warm fronts can bring warm, sunny weather.

When weather in an area suddenly changes, it is likely that a front has just passed. A passing front can cause strong winds. It also can cause storms.

Imagine a mass of cold, dry air. It moves into a mass of warm, wet air. The warm air rises above the cold air. As the warm air rises, it cools. The cooling air can no longer hold as much water. This water falls as rain. That is why it often storms along a cold front.

21

# A Cloudy Day

Clouds come in many shapes. Thin, wispy clouds may appear high in the sky.

Clouds sometimes look like gobs of whipped cream in the sky. Sometimes they look like soft feathers. But what are clouds?

Clouds are billions and billions of tiny drops of water or ice crystals bunched together. Some clouds are all water, some are all ice, and some are a mixture of each.

You might think the water and ice would be so heavy they would fall to the ground. But the drops are so tiny that the wind keeps them floating in the air.

Dark, tall clouds usually bring rain with them.

The water that makes clouds comes from Earth's surface. Every day, the sun heats up water on the surface. Some of this water changes from a liquid to a gas. The gas is called **water vapor.** Water vapor is invisible, like other gases in the air. Water vapor floats up into the air. As it rises higher and higher, the water vapor begins to cool. When it cools enough, water vapor turns back into liquid water. The water drops tend to form around bits of dust in the air. These tiny drops make up the clouds.

Moist, warm air

Sun rays

Damp earth

Light from the sun heats the ground and the air directly above it. The warm air becomes lighter and rises. As the air rises, it becomes cooler. If the air is moist, some water vapor condenses and forms clouds.

# Kinds of Clouds

There are many different kinds of clouds, and each kind has a name. Most kinds of clouds are named for their shape.

The clouds that look like great sheets pulled across the sky are called stratus (STRAY tuhs) clouds. These are the clouds that are closest to the ground. They form when a layer of warm air rolls over a layer of cooler air. Together, these layers form a thick, sheetlike cloud.

The clouds that look like fluffy balls of cotton or scoops of ice cream are called cumulus (kyoo myuh luhs) clouds. Cumulus clouds that rise high into the air may grow dark and heavy with rain. These are the clouds that cause thunderstorms.

The highest clouds of all look like thin, wispy streaks or curls. They are so high up in the air, where the air is cold, that they are made of ice droplets. These clouds are called cirrus (SIHR uhs) clouds.

Fog is a cloud that touches the ground instead of floating high in the sky. Like every other kind of cloud, fog forms when warm, moist air meets cool air.

The sunset can make clouds appear in different colors.

Cirrus clouds are high in the sky, where the air is cold. They are made of ice crystals.

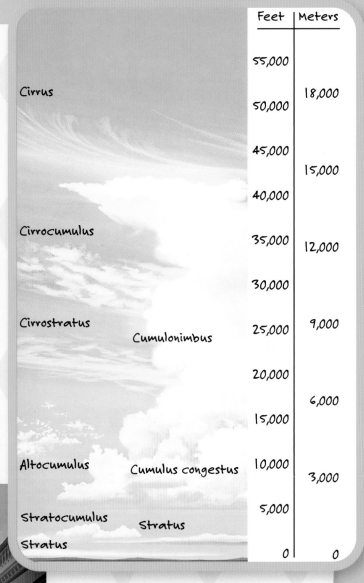

| Feet | Meters |
|---|---|
| 55,000 | |
| 50,000 | 18,000 |
| 45,000 | |
| | 15,000 |
| 40,000 | |
| 35,000 | 12,000 |
| 30,000 | |
| 25,000 | 9,000 |
| 20,000 | |
| | 6,000 |
| 15,000 | |
| 10,000 | 3,000 |
| 5,000 | |
| 0 | 0 |

Cirrus

Cirrocumulus

Cirrostratus

Cumulonimbus

Altocumulus     Cumulus congestus

Stratocumulus     Stratus

Stratus

Different types of clouds are seen at different heights above Earth.

Fog is a cloud that touches the ground. Fog often appears over bodies of water.

## Activity

# MAKE YOUR OWN CLOUD

Water is always present in the air around you, even when you can't see it or feel it. This experiment shows how clouds form when cold air and warm air come together.

## MATERIALS

- Drinking glass (made of glass or metal—not paper or plastic)
- Ice cubes
- Spoon

## DIRECTIONS

1. Do this experiment near a sink or a tub. While you work, run the hot water. This will ensure that there is much **water vapor** in the air around you.

2. Fill the glass halfway with cool water and dry the outside of the glass. Drop the ice cubes into the water and stir slowly. After a few minutes, feel the outside of the glass. Is it wet and cold?

H₂O

I Love science

What happened? The outside of the glass was dry before. Now the warmth from the running hot water has made the air wet nearby. The air is filled with water vapor. When some of this warm water vapor touched the cold glass, drops of water formed.

Clouds form in the same way. When warm air with water vapor in it meets cold air, clouds begin to form.

# A Rainy Day

Rain forms from droplets of water in clouds. When the droplets get heavy, they fall to the ground.

We know that clouds are made up of tiny water drops. These drops are small enough that the wind pushes them along through the air. So why does water fall from the sky as rain?

Under the right conditions, the drops of water in clouds can come together. As the drops get larger, they become heavier. Eventually, the drops become too heavy to remain in the air. The drops then fall to the ground as rain.

In the water cycle, water moves from the oceans to the air to the land and back to the oceans again.

1. The sun heats the ocean. This causes water from the ocean to turn into water vapor.

On a sunny day, turn your back to the sun. Spray a fine mist of water from a garden hose. You should see a rainbow in the shining spray. What colors do you see in the rainbow?

A rainbow is made by sunlight shining through drops of water. Sunlight looks white, but it is really made up of many colors. When sunlight enters a raindrop, it breaks up into its many colors. These colors are red, orange, yellow, green, blue, and violet.

Try this!

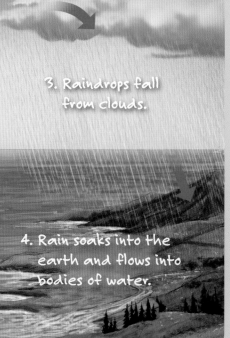

2. Water vapor forms clouds.

3. Raindrops fall from clouds.

4. Rain soaks into the earth and flows into bodies of water.

The water that falls as rain may soak into the ground. This water is used by plants. Also, people get most of their drinking water from water in the ground. Some of the water from rain flows into streams and rivers. This water eventually flows into the ocean. The sun can warm up the water in the ocean and turn it into a gas again. In this way, water is constantly moving from the ocean to the sky to the ground and back again. This movement is called the water cycle. Earth is always recycling its water.

# HOW MUCH RAIN FELL?

If you listen to a **meteorologist** (person who predicts weather) on the radio or television, you'll hear how many inches or centimeters of rain fell during a storm. How does the meteorologist know how much rain fell?

Scientists measure rainfall with an instrument called a rain gauge (gayj). Rain falls into the gauge. When the rain stops falling, scientists measure the amount of water in the gauge. You can make a simple rain gauge to measure the rainfall around your home.

## MATERIALS

- Large, clean jar with straight sides
- Ruler

## DIRECTIONS

1. On a rainy day, place the jar outdoors. Put it in an open place away from trees and buildings so that rain can fall directly into it.

2. Bury the jar partly in the ground or pile heavy rocks around it so that it can't move or tip.

3. Leave the jar outdoors until it rains. When the rain stops falling, carefully bring the jar indoors.

4. Hold the jar up and place the ruler along the side, with the lowest numbers at the bottom. Make sure the first mark on the ruler lines up with the bottom of the jar.

5. Read the ruler where the water line is. This will tell you how much rain has fallen. Record the amount in a journal or weather log.

6. Pour out the water, then dry the jar. Put the jar outside again for the next rainfall. Do you think it will rain more, less, or about the same amount as the first time you measured?

Each time the rain falls, people who study the weather record the amount. By keeping careful records, people can learn about weather patterns. These patterns help people predict how much rain will fall.

# A Snowy Day

Wet, heavy snow blankets trees, roads, and buildings.

Snow forms in much the same way as rain. It forms at the top of storm clouds where the air is cold. The cold air causes the water drops in clouds to freeze into ice crystals. The ice crystals grow in size as **water vapor** freezes onto them. A snowflake is actually a bunch of ice crystals frozen together.

When you look at a snowflake through a magnifying glass, you see a beautiful, lacy shape. No two snowflakes are exactly alike. Some have flat edges. Others have branching points. Most look like pieces of lace. Yet, in one way they are almost all the same. Nearly all snowflakes have six sides.

Snow can form high in the sky even in summer. But when snow falls in summer, it melts and becomes rain as it reaches warm air in the lower **atmosphere.**

A snowflake is made of crystals, or tiny pieces of frozen water.

By magnifying snowflakes, we can see their variety of shapes. ➤

Dry, powdery snow is perfect for skiing or snowboarding.

# Activity >

# MAKE YOUR OWN SNOWFLAKES

Snowflakes come in a seemingly endless variety of shapes. But nearly all snowflakes have six sides. Try this experiment to make your own snowflake.

## DIRECTIONS

1. Cut three segments of pipe cleaner into 4-inch (10-centimeter) lengths. Twist the segments together so that you have a six-sided snowflake.

2. Tie one end of string to one of the snowflake's branches near the center. Cut any excess string away from the knot. Wind the string around the branches until you have created two rows. Tie a knot. Be sure to leave some excess string to form a hanger for the snowflake. Tie this end of the string to a pencil.

I Love science

H₂O

3. Fill a large, deep container with boiling water. **Be sure to ask an adult to do this for you.** Mix the borax into the water. You should use about 3 tablespoons of borax for every cup of water. Stir the water until the borax is dissolved.

4. Place the snowflake in the solution. The pencil should rest on top of the container and the snowflake should not be touching the sides. Let the snowflake soak for at least 8 hours or longer.

## MATERIALS
- Pipe cleaners
- Ruler
- Scissors
- String
- Large, deep container
- Measuring cup
- Borax
- Boiling water
- Pencil
- Magnifying glass

5. Remove the snowflake and let it dry. You can use a magnifying glass to view the tiny crystals.

Lightning is a giant electrical spark that flows through the air. Some lightning travels within clouds and between clouds.

# Thunder and Lightning

A flash of light zigs and zags across the sky. Another flash zaps its way to the ground. A loud crack, boom, or rumble sounds soon after. The flash is lightning. The sound is thunder.

The flash we see when lightning snakes through the sky is a huge electric spark. During a thunderstorm, winds rub tiny water drops in the clouds against one another. This rubbing gives the water drops an electric charge. Soon, an entire cloud can have an electric charge. When this electric charge becomes strong enough, it forms a huge electric spark—lightning.

## Try this!

You can estimate the distance of a storm with this simple activity. When you see lightning, count the seconds before you hear the sound of thunder. Every five seconds equals about 1 mile (1.6 kilometers).

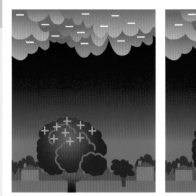 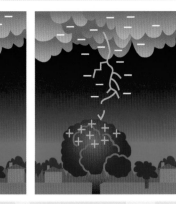 

Cloud-to-ground lightning is a release of electricity that begins in a cloud and strikes the ground.

Lightning can travel in many ways. Sometimes a charge flashes from one place to another within a cloud. Other times, electricity rushes between two clouds. Lightning can also strike the ground.

A flash of lightning heats the air to thousands of degrees. The heated air creates an explosion. Thunder is the sound of this explosion.

# HOW THUNDERSTORMS FORM

How do **fronts** of warm and cool air combine to create thunderstorms? This experiment will show you what happens when a storm gathers.

## MATERIALS

- Clear container about 6-8 inches (15-20 centimeters) long and a few inches deep, such as a glass baking dish or plastic food container

- Ice cube tray

- Small cup

- Dropper

- Food coloring (blue and red)

- Water

## DIRECTIONS

1. In the ice tray, make a blue ice cube by mixing 10 drops of blue food coloring with water. Place the ice cube tray in the freezer for several hours.

2. Fill the clear container with water. The water should be room temperature (it should not feel hot or cold when you stick your finger in it).

3. In the small cup, mix 10 drops of the red food coloring with warm water. The water should be warmer than the water in the container. The amount of water in the cup should be equivalent to the amount of water in the ice cube. Fill the dropper with the red water.

4. When the blue ice cube is frozen solid, place it in the water at one end of the container. Let it melt so that the blue coloring spreads toward the center of the container.

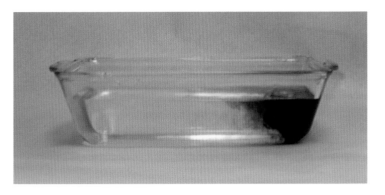

5. At the other end of the container, insert the dropper and gradually deposit the warm red water at the bottom of the container. Continue adding the red water so that it spreads to the center of the container.

The blue color represents cool air and the red color represents warm air. Now watch as the two fronts collide. What happens when they meet in the middle of the container?

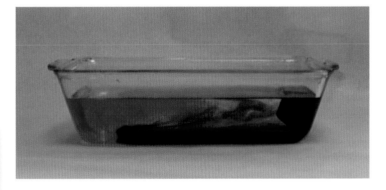

Prolonged, heavy rainstorms can cause areas to flood. In a severe flood, whole towns or cities may be damaged.

# Extreme Weather

Sometimes conditions in the **atmosphere** cause extreme weather. Extreme weather can be dangerous and do great damage.

During some severe storms, lumps of ice called hail or hailstones pound the ground. Hailstones are usually the size of little beads. But sometimes they are the size of golf balls or even larger!

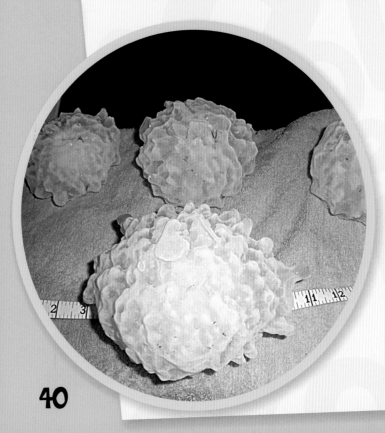

The largest hailstone ever recorded in the United States fell on July 23, 2010, in Vivian, South Dakota. It measured 8 inches (about 20 centimeters) wide.

Hailstones begin as frozen raindrops in a cloud. Wind keeps the frozen raindrops from falling to the ground. The frozen raindrops grow larger as more cold water freezes onto them. Finally, the hailstones become so heavy they fall. Hail can dent cars and break windows. It can even hurt people.

A blizzard is another kind of extreme weather. A blizzard is a blinding snowstorm with strong, cold winds. So much snow is blown around during a blizzard that it is hard to see. The snow can build up into deep drifts that make it hard to walk. A blizzard's icy winds can be dangerous for people and animals.

During a blizzard, people often stop driving and close businesses, schools, and other places.

Blizzards happen when cold air rushes into warm, moist air. This causes a violent storm and lots of snow.

# What Are Hurricanes?

A hurricane (HUHR uh kayn) is a huge, swirling storm. Hurricanes can be hundreds of miles or kilometers across. These storms have very powerful winds. They drop large amounts of rain. But in the center of all this wind and rain, the air is calm. This calm area is called the eye of the hurricane.

A hurricane begins over the ocean, near the **equator.** The air there is very hot and wet. This hot air rises, forming towering rain clouds. Surrounding air rushes in, causing strong winds. The rising air cools and sinks. Then it is drawn back in again. The entire storm begins to rotate around its center. This center forms the eye.

This **satellite** image shows Hurricane Katrina over the Gulf of Mexico. Katrina struck land on August 29, 2005.

In northern parts of the world, hurricane winds on the ocean surface swirl counterclockwise around a calm eye.

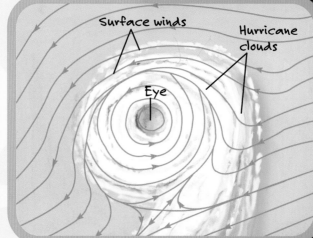

Surface winds

Hurricane clouds

Eye

42

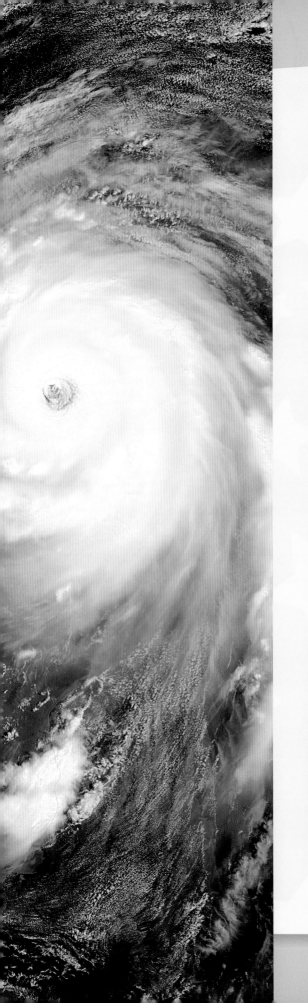

The winds become stronger and stronger. When the winds are stronger than 74 miles (119 kilometers) per hour, the storm has become a hurricane.

When hurricanes reach land, they can do horrible damage. The winds smash trees and wreck homes. Hurricanes also cause flooding. These storms can be very dangerous. The eye sometimes tricks people into leaving shelters too early. They think the storm has passed. Then the other side of the hurricane hits, doing even more damage.

Hurricanes can cause much destruction. This home near Biloxi, Mississippi, was damaged by Hurricane Katrina in 2005.

# MAKE YOUR OWN BAROMETER

A **barometer** is an instrument that measures **air pressure**. A change in air pressure usually means that the weather will soon change. In general, cloudy weather occurs in low-pressure areas. Clear weather occurs in high-pressure areas.

## MATERIALS

- Balloon
- 2 jars of the same size
- Rubber bands
- Drinking straw
- Glue
- Flat toothpick
- Pencil
- Scissors
- Craft stick

## DIRECTIONS

1. Cut off the open end of a balloon. Stretch the rest of the balloon over the top of a jar. Fasten the balloon onto the jar with a rubber band.

2. Flatten the straw and cut one end into a point. Glue the other end to the center of the balloon.

3. Glue a toothpick to the balloon at the edge of the jar. The straw should lie on the toothpick. The straw is the barometer's "needle."

4. Attach a craft stick to the outside of the other jar with a couple of rubber bands so that it reaches about 1 inch (2.5 centimeters) above the top. If your craft stick doesn't have markings like a ruler, add them along one side, top to bottom.

5. Place the jars so that the cut end of the straw points to the craft stick.

6. Check your barometer at the same time every day. Does it point to a higher or lower mark than the day before? Higher marks mean lower air pressure. Lower marks mean higher air pressure.

You can use your barometer to keep track of the weather over time. Ask an adult for a calendar you can write on. Create symbols for the weather. For example, a wiggly line can be clouds, a smiling face can be sunshine. Each day, record the pressure and draw symbols for the day's weather on the calendar.

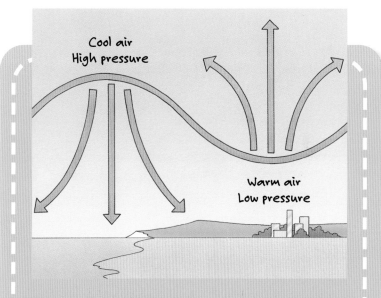

Cool air
High pressure

Warm air
Low pressure

The pressure made by air is related to the temperature of the air. Warm air weighs less than cool air. So where the air is warmer, the air pressure is lower. Where the air is cooler, the air pressure is higher. Warm, light air rises and cool, heavy air sinks.

# What Are Tornadoes?

A tornado is a cone-shaped tube of air that swirls with high-speed winds.

A towering dark cloud approaches. Heavy rain falls, and then hail. The sky turns an eerie shade of green. Suddenly, a spinning tube comes down to the ground. When this funnel touches the ground, dirt and debris fly through the air. Entire houses are lifted from the ground. A tornado (tawr NAY doh) has landed.

Tornadoes are the most violent storms. Their winds can reach 300 miles (480 kilometers) per hour. Few buildings can survive the strongest tornadoes. People must take shelter underground.

Thundercloud

Rain and hail

Wall cloud

Funnel

A tornado forms after a low, heavy cloud called a wall cloud takes shape under a large thundercloud. The rapidly swirling funnel comes out of the wall cloud and touches the ground. Rain and hail may fall from the thundercloud.

Tornadoes happen when two **fronts** meet. Air that is high up moves in one direction. Air that is lower down moves in a different direction. This causes part of the storm to spin on its side. If the spinning air gets turned upright, a tornado can reach down toward the ground.

Tornadoes can happen in many parts of the world. But most tornadoes happen in the central United States in an area called Tornado Alley.

In April 2011, more than 200 tornadoes broke out across the southern United States in less than a week. Above, a journalist walks through a destroyed neighborhood in Tuscaloosa, Alabama.

## Activity >

# MAKE YOUR OWN TORNADO

Tornadoes are the most violent types of storms, with winds that can swirl at speeds up to 300 miles (480 kilometers) per hour. A tornado forms when rotating air at the bottom of a thundercloud moves toward the ground. Here is a simple experiment that shows how tornado winds swirl.

## DIRECTIONS

1. Remove the screw-top lids from the two bottles. Glue the tops of the lids together. **Ask an adult to help you punch or drill a hole the size of a drinking straw through the middle of the lids.**

2. Put several small bits of paper into one of the bottles.

3. Fill the same bottle about three-fourths full of water.

4. Screw the lids onto the full bottle. Then screw the empty bottle on top. Make sure that the lids are screwed tightly and that the seal is waterproof.

5. Turn the bottles over so that the one with water and paper bits is on top. Spin them so that the water starts to rotate inside. As the water twists down into the empty bottle, the air will rise up through the water in the top bottle and look just like a tornado. The paper bits should make your "tornado" easy to see.

## MATERIALS

- 2 large plastic soft-drink bottles with screw-top lids
- Strong glue
- Hole punch or drill
- Confetti or other small bits of paper

The air in the bottle represents warm air rising to form a tornado. Try turning the bottle upside down without spinning it. You'll see that the water does not flow through the hole very easily when the bottle is not spinning.

# Weather Watchers

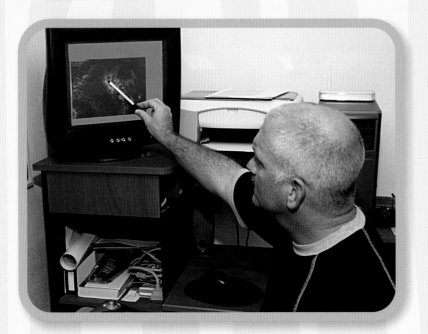

A meteorologist tracks a hurricane using a satellite image.

A weather balloon can carry instruments that measure air temperature, humidity, and air pressure high in the sky. .

A **meteorologist** (mee tee uh RAHL uh jihst) is a scientist who studies Earth's **atmosphere** and its weather. Meteorologists predict the weather.

How do meteorologists predict the weather? They check the wind's speed and direction. They record the temperature of the air, the **air pressure,** and the amount of water in the air.

Meteorologists also gather information from weather **satellites** (SAT uh lytz) in outer space. These satellites circle Earth and photograph clouds and storms. The pictures are then sent back to Earth.

A scientist adjusts a tool designed to measure the winds inside a tornado.

A researcher checks the weather instruments aboard a buoy in the Pacific Ocean. The instruments measure ocean temperatures at different depths. They also provide information about wind direction and speed.

↓

Information also comes from weather stations on Earth's surface. A machine called Doppler radar uses radio waves to track storms. It can spot storms that are more than 200 miles (320 kilometers) away.

Meteorologists gather weather reports from all over the world. They use this information to draw weather maps. They also use computers to make **forecasts** (FAWR kastz). You hear their forecasts on television, over the radio, or on the Internet. But since the weather can change quickly, meteorologists often update their forecasts.

# MAKE YOUR OWN HYGROMETER

**Meteorologists** measure the amount of moisture in the air with an instrument called a hygrometer (hy GROM uh tuhr). This instrument is used in weather stations on the ground or in aircraft, ships, and weather balloons. Meteorologists use the information from the hygrometer to **forecast** the weather.

One of the simplest types of hygrometer is the hair hygrometer. It uses human hairs to measure humidity. You can make your own hair hygrometer. Keep a chart of your results every day for three weeks. Can you forecast whether it will be wet or dry during the fourth week?

## MATERIALS

- Ruler
- Pen or pencil
- Scissors
- Piece of thin cardboard, 6 inches x 1.5 inches (15 centimeters x 4 centimeters)
- Tape
- Strand of hair, about 8 inches (20 centimeters) long
- Piece of stiff cardboard, 8.5 inches x 11 inches (21 centimeters x 27.5 centimeters)
- 6 thumbtacks
- Piece of wood, 11 inches x 2 inches x 2 inches (27.5 centimeters x 5 centimeters x 5 centimeters)
- Colored pen with a fine point

## DIRECTIONS

1. Using the ruler, draw an arrow about 5 inches by 1 inch (12.5 centimeters by 2.5 centimeters) on the thin cardboard. Cut out the arrow.

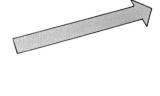

2. Tape one end of the strand of hair to the center-top of the stiff cardboard.

3. Using thumbtacks, attach the cardboard to the long edge of the piece of wood.

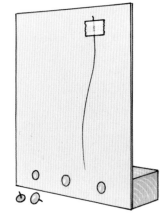

4. Attach the free end of the hair to the middle of the back of the arrow.

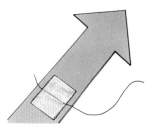

5. Place the arrow against the cardboard and move it until the hair is stretched out fully and also parallel to the long side of the cardboard. Then attach the end of the arrow (opposite the arrowhead) to the cardboard with a thumbtack.

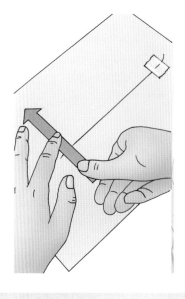

6. Stand the hygrometer outside. Make sure that it can't fall over. When the sun is shining, with the colored pen, mark on the cardboard where the arrow is pointing. Write "dry" by the side of this mark. When the weather is damp, the arrow will point lower. Mark its new position and write "damp" on the cardboard.

On damp days, the strand of hair will absorb moisture from the air. This will make the hair stretch, causing the arrow to point lower. On dry, sunny days, the hair dries out and becomes shorter.

Spring

Summer

# What Causes Seasons?

In summer, trees burst with green leaves. Warm breezes blow. In winter, bare trees stand like bony skeletons. In some places, snow blankets the ground.

Why is it warm in the summer and cold in the winter? The answer has to do with sunlight. In the summer, the days are long. The sun shines brightly. In the winter, the days are short. The sun shines weakly.

We know that Earth spins like a top. That is why we have days and nights. But Earth is tilted in relation to the sun. This tilt causes different parts of Earth to receive more sunlight during different parts of the year.

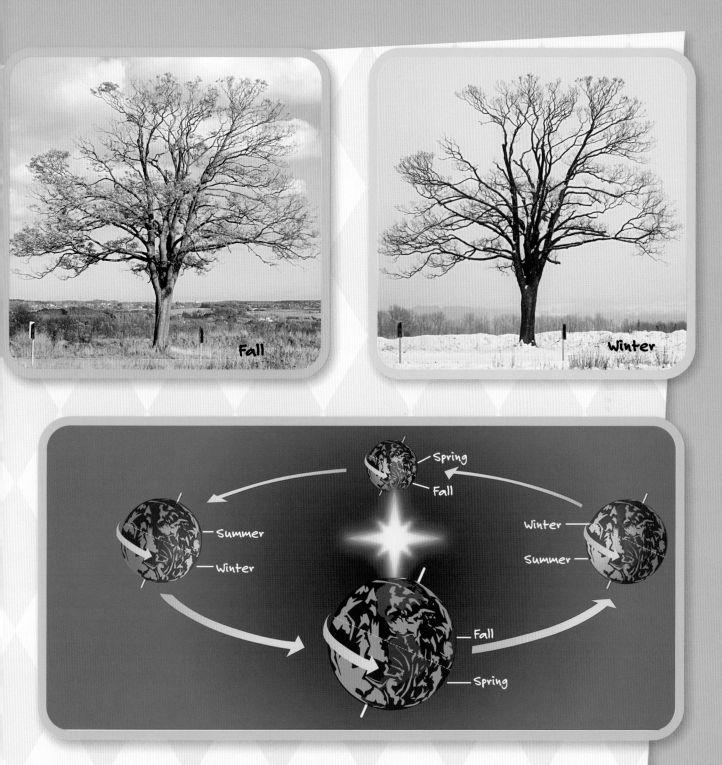

Fall

Winter

Spring
Fall

Summer
Winter

Winter
Summer

Fall

Spring

When the northern part of Earth is tilted toward the sun, it is summer there. On the other side of the world, it is winter. When the northern part of Earth is tilted away from the sun, it is winter there. It is summer on the southern side.

The northern and southern parts of Earth both have seasons, but they occur at opposite times.

# What Is Climate?

Desert areas have hot, dry climates year-round.

Some places are warm almost every day of the year. Other places are mostly cool and rainy. Still other places have changing seasons, with cold winters and hot summers.

**Climate** (KLY miht) is what the weather is like in the same area over a long period of time. Climate is different from weather. Weather is what happens in the **atmosphere** over a short period of time. Climate happens over long periods.

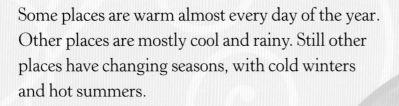

The polar regions are always cold. They are covered in snow and ice all or most of the year.

The sun, the ocean, and the land all influence climate. At the North and South poles, the climate is cold because there is little sunlight. Near the **equator,** the climate is warm because there is much sunlight.

Warm areas near the ocean tend to have the wettest climates. Huge rain forests can grow in these places.

Mountains usually have a cooler climate than the land around them. When wet air climbs over a mountain, it cools. Heavy rains may fall. By the time the air reaches the other side of the mountain, it is very dry. A desert may form in that area.

Tropical rain forests are warm and wet. They are home to more different kinds of plants and animals than anywhere else in the world.

Try this!

How would you describe the climate of the area where you live? One way to learn about your climate is to research what the weather is like over long periods. At your local library, look up the weather report for this date last year. What was the weather like 5 years ago? 10 years? 50 years? What's similar about the weather over time and what's different?

# A Warming Earth

Earth is slowly getting warmer. Most scientists believe that people are causing this change. The reason is that human activities are releasing **greenhouse gases.** But what is a greenhouse gas?

Have you ever seen a greenhouse? It has glass walls that let in light so plants can grow. Because the walls also hold in heat, a greenhouse becomes very warm.

The greenhouse effect describes how gases in Earth's atmosphere trap heat. This heat warms the land, the oceans, and the air.

## Try this!

**Climate** scientists have found that our planet is slowly becoming warmer. The National Aeronautics and Space Administration (NASA) has a website that describes the evidence for global warming. You can visit the website at http://climate.nasa.gov/evidence. Name at least two pieces of evidence for global warming. How do you think these changes could affect people in years to come?

Factories release harmful chemicals and other materials that damage the air, water, and land.

Cars and other vehicles burn fuels that release harmful gases into the atmosphere.

Earth and its **atmosphere** act like a greenhouse. Light from the sun passes through the atmosphere and warms Earth. Much of this heat escapes back into space. But greenhouse gases in the atmosphere act like the glass in a greenhouse. They trap some of the heat.

Cars, factories, and power plants burn fuels that release greenhouse gases. Unfortunately, people are adding so many greenhouse gases to the atmosphere that temperatures are climbing. Many scientists fear that Earth will become much warmer in the next 100 years. This problem is called **global warming.**

# How Can We Protect Earth?

For thousands of years, people have used Earth's land, water, and air. People have also damaged Earth with their garbage and **pollution** (harmful chemicals or waste).

Now, people all over the world are working to protect Earth. They are working to preserve land, reduce pollution, save natural resources, and protect endangered wildlife. There are many ways to help Earth. You can help, too.

With these three R's—reduce, reuse, and recycle—you can help preserve Earth's resources.

Such simple activities as picking up garbage in a park may encourage others to help protect Earth.

Encouraging family members to ride bikes or walk instead of driving cars can help reduce pollution.

## REDUCE

- Use fewer paper and plastic products. Use cloth towels instead of paper towels.

- Turn off the lights, radio, and TV when you're not using them.

- Instead of running water until it's cold, keep a pitcher of cold water in the refrigerator.

- To save hot water, take showers instead of baths.

- If your family has a dishwasher, don't use it until you have a full load.

- Ride a bike, join a carpool, or take the bus or train to save on gas and oil.

## REUSE

- Wash out plastic milk bottles, plastic bags, and aluminum foil, and reuse them.

- Repair and reuse toys and other products.

- Save used paper and plastic to make gifts.

- Use both sides of writing paper.

- Sell or donate goods so someone else can reuse them.

## RECYCLE

- Recycle aluminum cans, glass and plastic containers, newspapers, rubber items, and paper. Recycled materials are used to make new products.

- Use recycled paper to write, paint, and draw.

# Glossary

**air pressure** the weight of air pressing down from above.

**atmosphere** the gases that surround Earth or any other planet.

**barometer** a device that measures air pressure.

**climate** the typical weather of a place. Climate includes the temperature, amount of rain or snow, winds, and other conditions in an area.

**equator** an imaginary line that circles the middle of Earth. It is halfway between the North Pole and the South Pole.

**forecast** to tell what is going to happen before it happens. A weather forecast lets people know what kind of weather is coming.

**front** the boundary separating two different air masses.

**global warming** an increase in the average temperature at Earth's surface.

**greenhouse gas** a gas that warms the atmosphere by trapping heat from the sun.

**meteorologist** a person who studies climate and forecasts weather.

**molecule** a group of joined atoms. A molecule is the smallest piece a compound can be broken into and still stay the same.

**pollution** harmful chemicals and other materials that people make that damage the air, water, and land.

**satellite** a vehicle in outer space that circles Earth. Many satellites observe the weather.

**thermometer** an instrument for measuring temperature.

**water vapor** water in the form of a gas.

# Find Out More

## Books

**Fluffy, Flat, and Wet: A Book About Clouds** by Dana Meachen Rau and Denise Shea (Picture Window Books, 2006)

**Global Warming** by Seymour Simon (Collins, 2010)

**Storms** by Miriam Goin (National Geographic, 2009)

**Weather** by Lorrie Mack (DK Publishing, 2004)

**What Happens in Winter?** by Sara L. Latta (Enslow Publishers, 2006)

**What's the Weather?** by Melissa Stewart (Compass Point Books, 2005)

## Websites

**Edheads: Weather**
http://www.edheads.org/activities/weather
Interactive games and activities at this website will help you predict and report on the weather.

**FEMA for Kids**
http://www.fema.gov/kids/
This website from the Federal Emergency Management Agency (FEMA) teaches what you need to know about all kinds of weather emergencies, from hurricanes to winter storms.

**Franklin's Forecast**
http://sln.fi.edu/weather/
Become "weatherwise" at this website from The Franklin Institute.

**Ice and Snow**
http://www.units.muohio.edu/dragonfly/snow/
Learn about the different characteristics of snow and ice at this educational website, created by researchers in Antarctica.

**NOAA's National Severe Storms Laboratory: Albums**
http://www.photolib.noaa.gov/nssl/index.html
Look through photo albums of stormy skies, hailstorms, tornadoes, and lightning at this site from the National Oceanic and Atmospheric Administration (NOAA).

**Sky Diary: Kidstorm**
http://skydiary.com/kids/
What causes tornadoes? How can you stay safe in a lightning storm? Learn about storms and storm chasers at this educational website.

**Weather WizKids**
http://www.weatherwizkids.com/
Information on all kinds of weather, from seasons to storms, is available at this website from meteorologist Crystal Wicker.

**Web Weather for Kids**
http://eo.ucar.edu/webweather/
Check out weather-related games, stories, and activities at this site. Includes a tutorial on making your own weather predictions.

# Index

# Activities